CHRISTMAS SONGS
FOR CLASSICAL PLAYERS

T0088349

ISBN 978-1-4950-9879-6

To access companion recorded piano accompaniments online, visit:
www.halleonard.com/mylibrary

Enter Code
8724-6695-1895-9557

HAL•LEONARD®

7777 W. BLUEMOUND RD. P.O. BOX 13819 MILWAUKEE, WI 53213

Visit Hal Leonard Online at
www.halleonard.com

Pianists on the recordings: [1] Brendan Fox, [2] Richard Walters

The price of this publication includes access to companion recorded piano accompaniments online,
for download or for streaming, using the unique code found on the title page.
Visit **www.halleonard.com/mylibrary** and enter the access code.

The Christmas Song
(Chestnuts Roasting on an Open Fire)

Music and Lyric by Mel Tormé
and Robert Wells
Arranged by Richard Walters

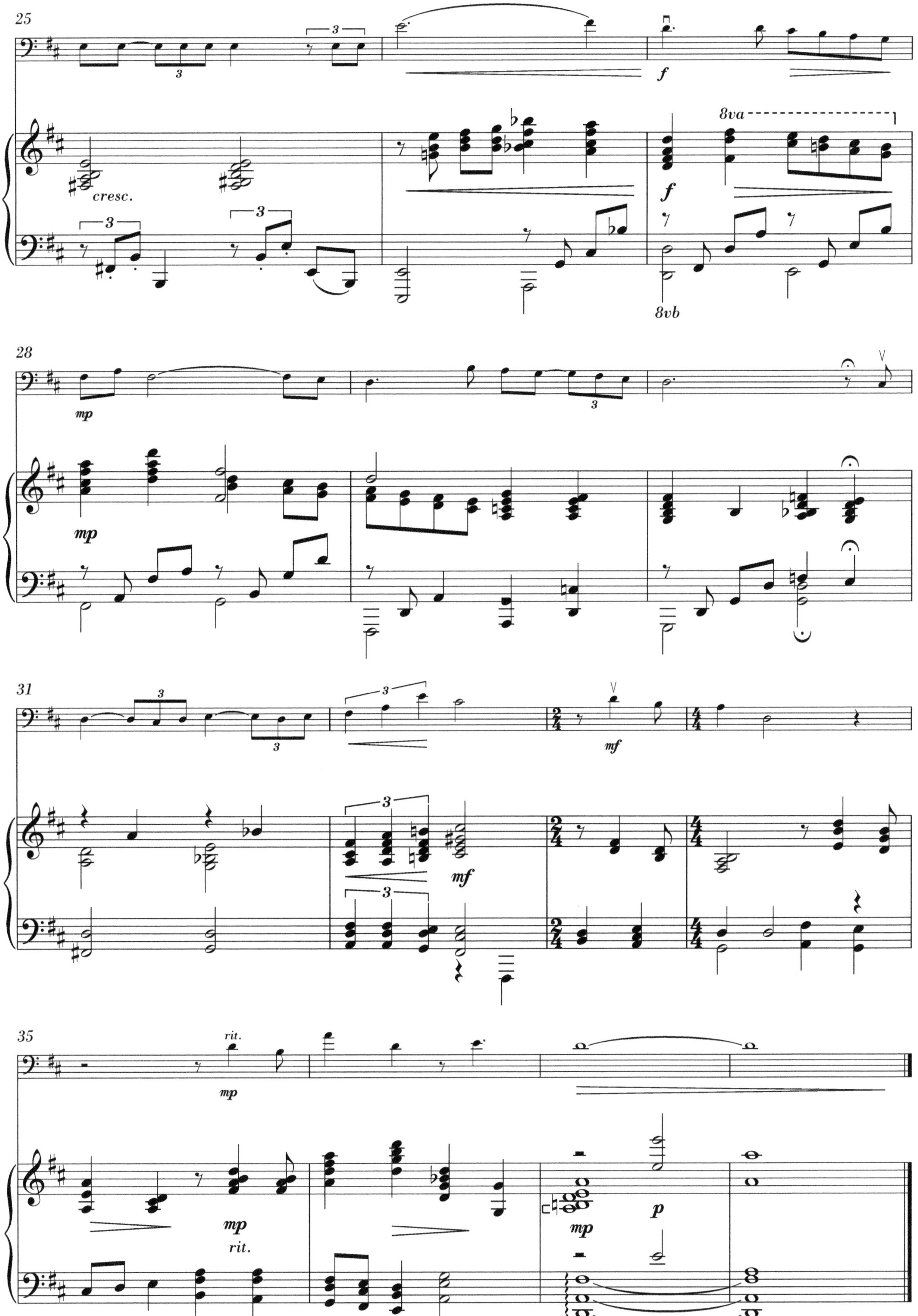
25
cresc.
f
8va
8vb
28
mp
31
mf
35
rit.
mp
p

Christmas Time Is Here
from A CHARLIE BROWN CHRISTMAS

Words by Lee Mendelson
Music by Vince Guaraldi
Arranged by Joshua Parman

The Christmas Waltz

Words by Sammy Cahn
Music by Jule Styne
Arranged by Hank Powell

Moderate Waltz

Have Yourself a Merry Little Christmas

from MEET ME IN ST. LOUIS

Words and Music by Hugh Martin
and Ralph Blane
Arranged by Celeste Avery

The Most Wonderful Time of the Year

Words and Music by Eddie Pola
and George Wyle
Arranged by Luke Duane

Brightly, in one

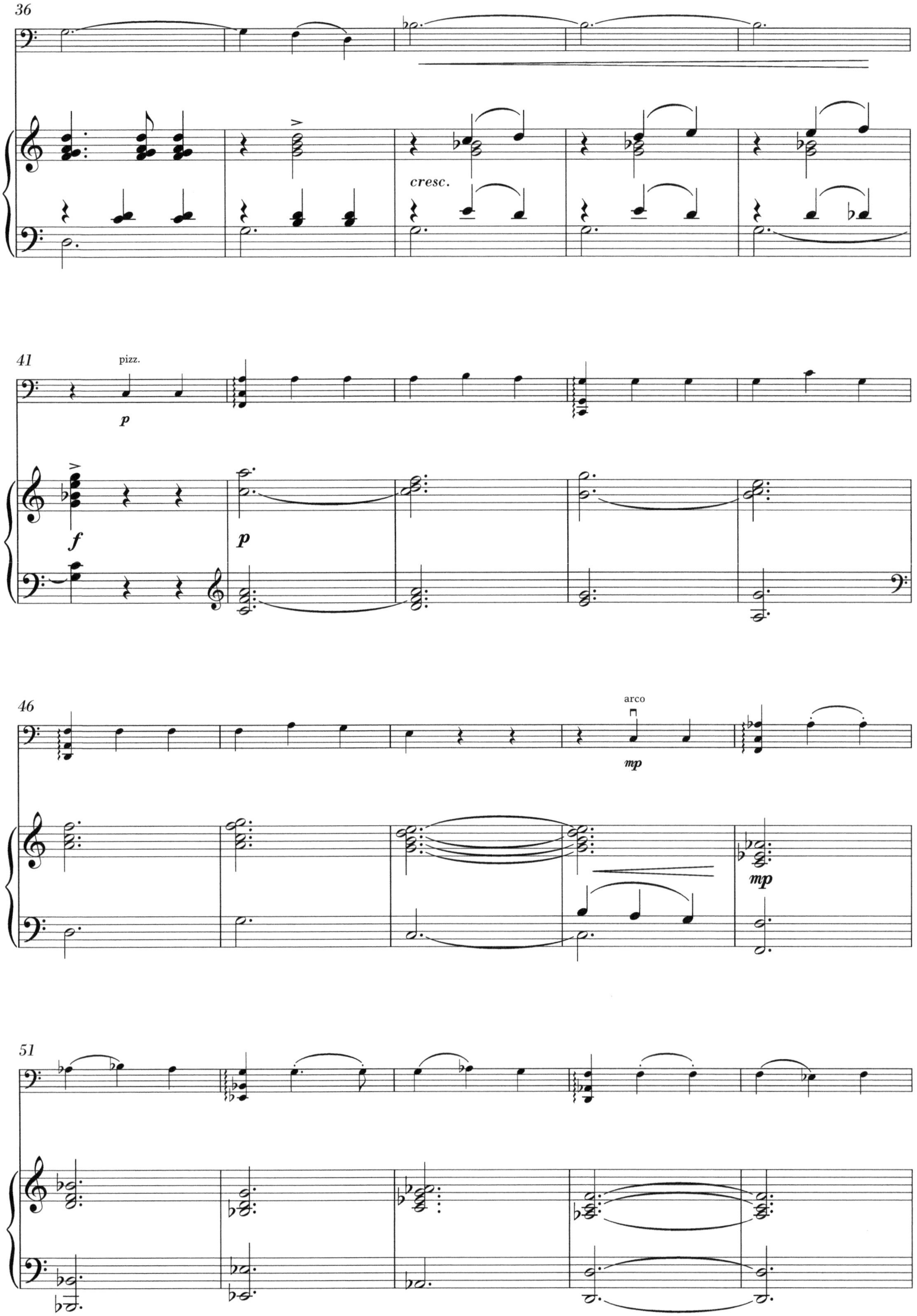
36
cresc.
41
pizz.
p
f
p
46
arco
mp
mp
51

I Wonder As I Wander
(Appalachian Carol)

By John Jacob Niles
Adapted and arranged by Celeste Avery

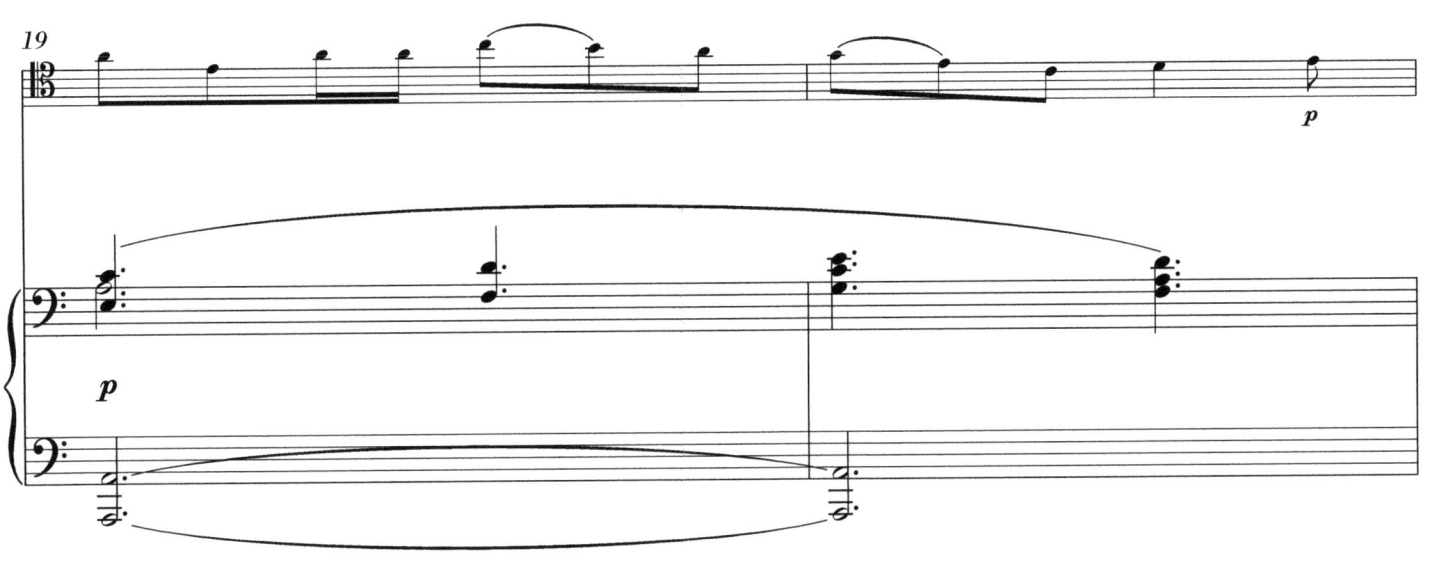

I'll Be Home for Christmas

Words and Music by Kim Gannon
and Walter Kent
Arranged by Brendan Fox

Moderately slow

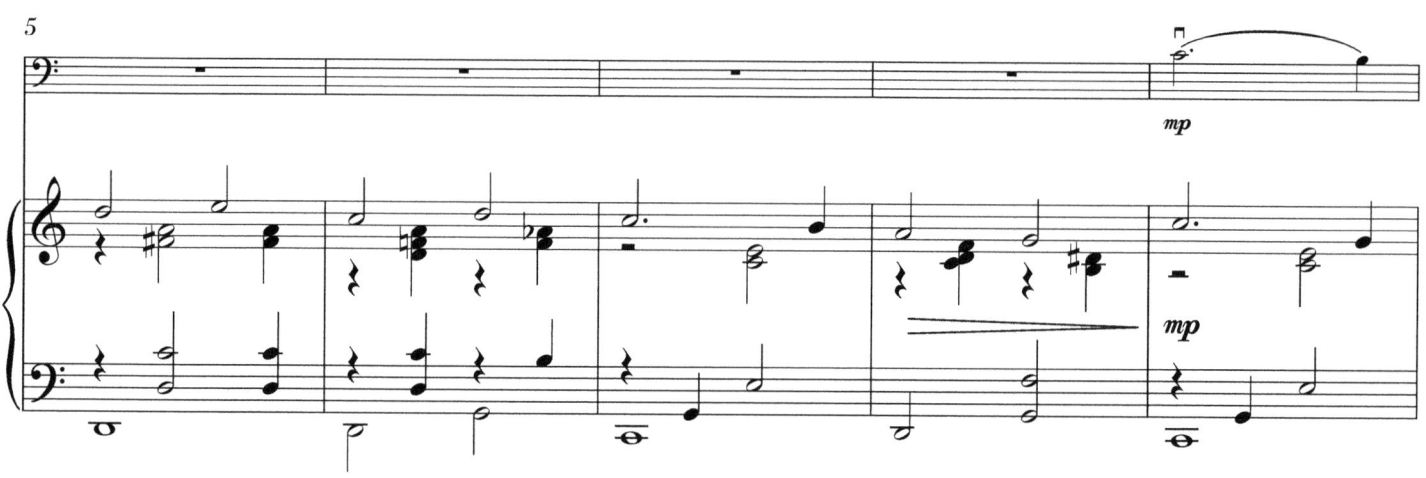

O Christmas Tree
(O Tannenbaum)

16th century Silesian folksong
Arranged by Richard Walters

Sleigh Ride

Music by Leroy Anderson
Arranged by Celeste Avery

Silver Bells
from the Paramount Picture THE LEMON DROP KID

Words and Music by Jay Livingston
and Ray Evans
Arranged by Luke Duane

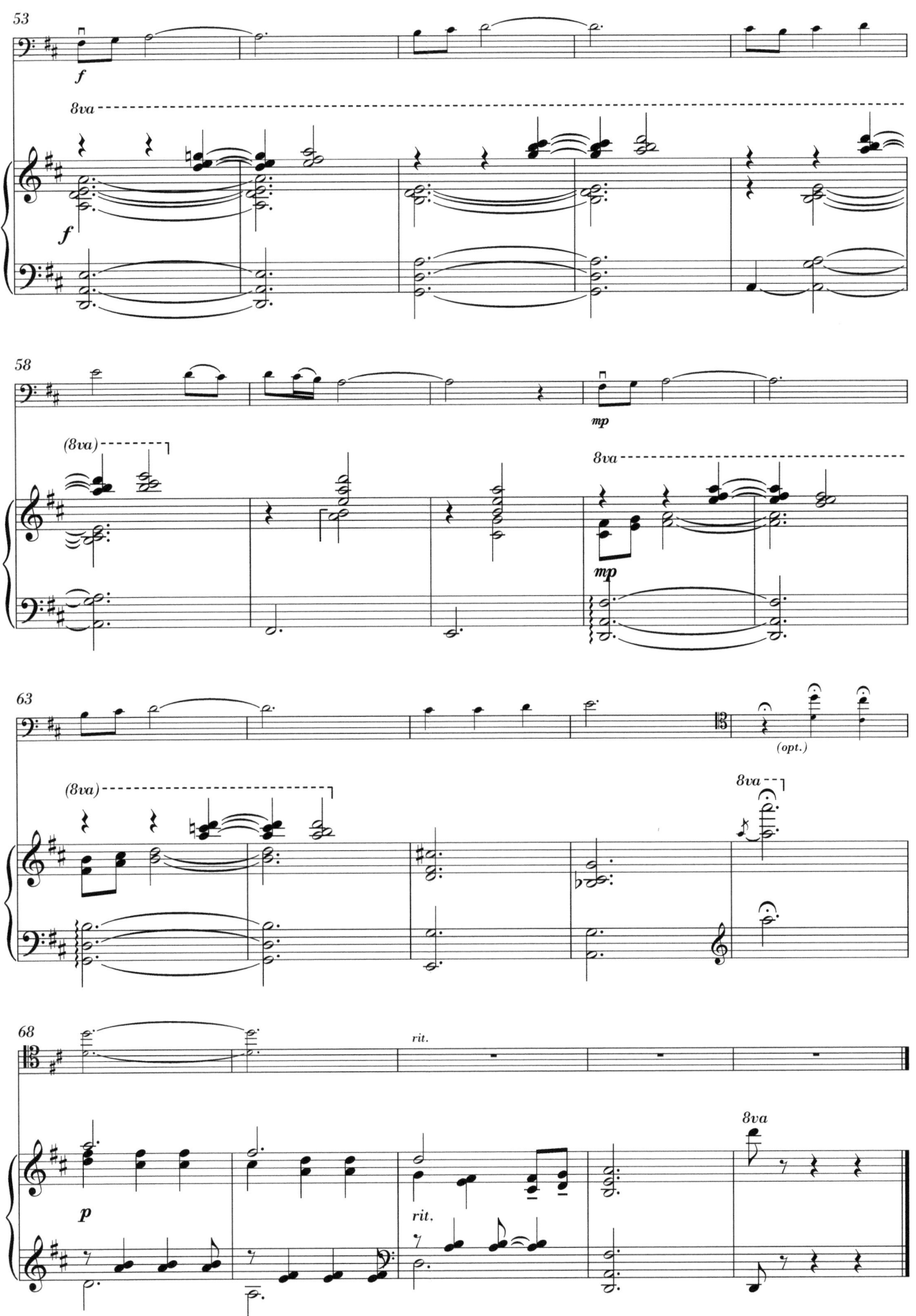

White Christmas

from the Motion Picture Irving Berlin's HOLIDAY INN

Words and Music by
Irving Berlin
Arranged by Richard Walters

Moderately, expressively

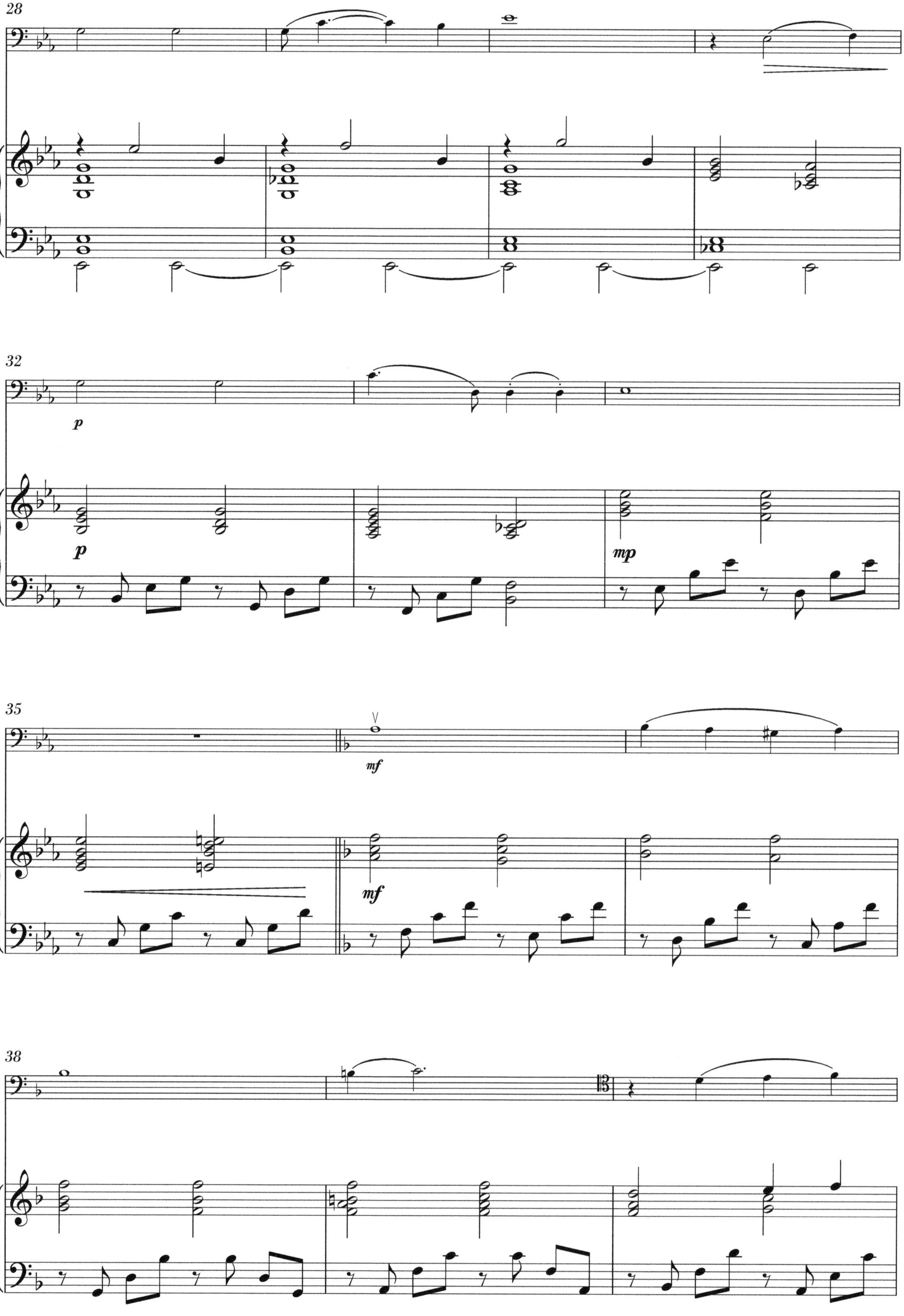
28
32
p
p
mp
35
mf
mf
38

Waltz of the Flowers
from *The Nutcracker*

Pyotr Il'yich Tchaikovsky
Arranged by Joshua Parman

Tempo di Valse